TOTNES REMEMBERED

Compiled by Totnes Museum Society

An aerial photograph about 1920 before the development off Station Road. The old market and Lion Brewery are on the right.

This version of the book is virtually as originally published, presenting the work of the Totnes Museum Society. There are now additional pages at the back providing information about the publisher, Arthur L Clamp.

The republishing project is being managed by Arthur's grandson, Steven Gibson. We aim to find all the research that he was involved in publishing, preserving it for the next generation as part of 'The Clamp Collection'.

INTRODUCTION

I am indebted to Mr. A. L. Clamp and to Miss Jean Bell, Custodian of the Elizabethan House Museum, Totnes, for the opportunity of providing a brief introduction to the collection of annotated illustrations of the ancient borough of Totnes. The majority of the photographs used are in the Museum collections, but we are most grateful also to Mrs. E. Hillier, Mr. Hodder, George Heath and the Dart Rowing Club for providing others.

Totnes is, of course, of considerable antiquity and the ground plan, still recognisable, of the original town is that of the Saxon burgh of King Alfred. The Normans added the motte and bailey castle which still exists, but the oval shape of the stockaded Saxon settlement was retained throughout medieval and later times, with an eastward extension down to the river crossing and the formation of a suburb (Bridgetown) on the further bank.

Naturally, little survives of the earlier periods, but from Elizabethan times onward there are fine examples of urban architecture with a refreshing variety of styles along the whole length of the principal streets (High Street and Fore Street).

Totnes, once a quiet market town, has now become a tourist attraction, with the inevitable result that publicity "gimmicks" attract the less observant visitor. However, the town has not lost its charm for those who are genuinely interested in the past, and to them this book is dedicated.

To obtain the maximum benefit from its use, it is suggested that a study of the illustrations should be followed by a walk around the town to compare the old photographs with the present scene. Although some of the places depicted have been demolished or altered beyond recognition, it is still possible to identify many of the subjects and to consider whether time has brought about an improvement. Such considerations lead very obviously to the merits or otherwise of conservation and to an understanding of the very considerable problems which have to be faced in a town with so much that is worthy of preservation.

The photographs reproduced here are, of course, related to comparatively recent times but still give an interesting insight into life in Totnes in the eighteenth, nineteenth and early twentieth centuries, and will revive many memories of times past.

E. N. Masson Phillips,
President of Totnes Museum Society,
Totnes, May, 1981.

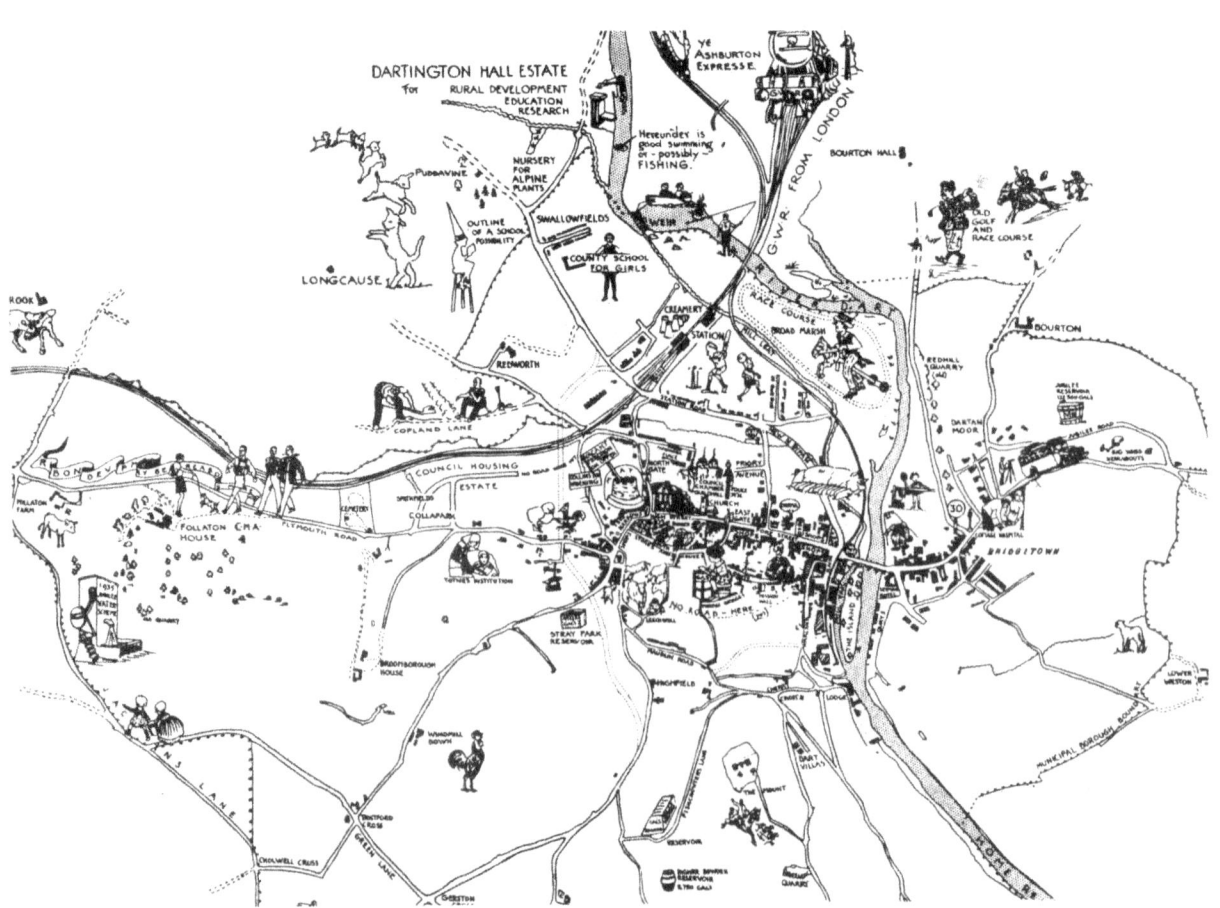

The Guildhall before alterations in 1878 and the old Grammar School. In 1850, about ten years before this photograph was taken, the master was ordered not to charge more than six guineas each per annum to the day scholars for a classical education. The number of boys increased from 20 to 50 when the school moved to the Mansion in 1887.

Golden wedding photograph of Mary Jane (nee Salter) and Stephen Clark married in Totnes in 1858. The Salters originally came from Berry Pomeroy and were living at 11 Moorashes in 1851. Stephen, a sailor from Malborough, had been shipwrecked off the Spanish coast and believed dead but he returned overland, taking six months to do so.

The Taunton Monument, also known as the Castle and Keys, was erected at the end of New Walk when a new bowling green was opened there in 1824, during the mayoralty of William Doidge Taunton. The monument was at the end of an avenue of trees planted between 1784 and 1795 to the north of the Steam Packet Inn.

An early paddle steamer at St. Peter's Quay in 1859. Charles Seale Hayne and some other gentlemen bought the paddle tug *Pilot* from a company in South Shields. She became the first unit of the Dartmouth Steam Packet Company and ran summer excursions as far as the Channel Islands. The regular steamers in the 1860s called at Greenway, Dittisham and Duncannon.

The launching of the Dart Rowing Club's new boat in 1914 named *Totnesia* by the Mayor, Councillor E. Windeatt. The group includes T. H. Chenhall, *Captain*, F. Tozer, *Cox*, G. H. Kirk, *Sub-Captain* and the Junior Crew (in front of the boat), S. Phillips, B. Stephens, Tozer, *Cox*, W. Lappage and H. Hitt.

A busy scene at the landing stage in 1907 with "Boats for hire, without man, 6d-1s per hour, 5s per day; with man, 1s 6d first hour, 1s an hour after". Steamer fares to Dartmouth were single 1/6 and return 2/6. Cycles 1/- and Motor Cycles 2/- each way.

Town Mills. The building in the foreground still stands but the wheel has gone; the stone building in the background was built as a granary in the Crimean War. The mills were bought by the West of England Bacon Company in 1918. The miller, William Cole, lived in Mill Lane. The mill was in use until 1945.

There were five inns in Bridgetown in the middle of the 19th century; William Farley, a thin man known as *Billy Fat*, kept the Bridge Inn. The Ale-Taster of the Bridgetown Court Leet made an annual tour of the pubs and stood outside with one foot on the pavement and one in the gutter to test his pint of beer.

A view of High Street taken before the clock was installed in the East Gate, the clock struck its first hour at noon on 9th August, 1880. The Gate House had been purchased by Lord Seymour in 1850 and it was opened as a Mechanics' Institute and Reading Room. The footpaths were flagged and the houses numbered in 1877.

Beating the Bounds in 1905. The beaters were ferried across the river from Seymour Hutch (the grandstand of the race course is in the background) to reach the next boundary stone at the bridge below Chateau Bellevue. One of the main objects of the exercise, for the boys, was to splash everyone as thoroughly as possible without themselves falling into the river.

The shop front of Henry Collins, baker and confectioner of 22 High Street, in 1902. John Frederick Ellis had been a baker and chocolate maker there from 1857 to 1890.

A group at Follaton Lodge during Beating the Bounds in 1905. A refreshment waggon was on hand with buns, bread and cheese and lemonade provided by the mayor. General high spirits were the order of the day — orchards were plundered, apple battles ensued and the more intrepid wormed their way through "buttle" (drainage) holes in the hedges.

Band of "C" Company, 5th Volunteer Battalion of the Devonshire Regiment in 1897 played at Dart View by invitation of Captain T. W. Windeatt, with Sergeant Instructor Furzeman and the non-commissioned officers of the Company. Bandsmen, under supervision of G. Loam, were E. Cuming, W. Doble, F. Heath, C. and H. Kinsman, T. Light, S. Reed, F. Stephens, F. D. and G. Tapley, A. Toope and Bugler H. Budd.

The Town Crier and Bill Poster, Arthur Benjamin Niner, was known as *Peeky Niner* and used to run a clothing store in High Street. He is remembered as going round, before the First World War, ringing his bell to publicise sales, meetings, sports events and even election results.

Market days were very busy in Totnes with the farmers driving by pony and trap laden with produce. The horses were kept in the local inns all of which could provide stabling. The house to the right of the Seven Stars was Portland House (later the Old Oak Cafe) which was demolished in 1936.

In the procession for Queen Victoria's Jubilee in 1887 were two model ships in separate conveyances in the charge of Mr. Thomas and driven by Messrs. Heath, Blake and Stabb in the employ of Mr. Stigings, coal merchant, The Quay, which attracted much interest.

Queen Victoria's Jubilee, 1897. The Procession, which was a grand spectacle, over half a mile in length, assembled on the Plains. The Volunteers headed by the Band with Captain Windeatt in command marched up shortly after 11 a.m. On the arrival of the Mayor a brilliant signal, specially written by Mr. C. L. Loam, Bandmaster, was given by five cornets and a rattling "feu de joie" was fired.

Jubilee 1897. The Mayor's Carriage, supplied by the Seymour Hotel, was drawn by four horses with Messrs. Rumbelow and E. Clarke attired in scarlet coat and white breeches acting as postillions. In the carriage were: the Mayor (Mr. T. C. Kellock), Rev. T. H. Elliott (Vicar of Totnes), Messrs. H. Symons (Deputy Mayor) and E. Windeatt (Town Clerk).

Interior of the Parish Church before the restoration which began in 1867 with Sir Gilbert Scott as adviser. The sounding board over the pulpit had two "pineapples" which were removed and hung on the front of 51 High Street. The old box pews were also taken away. The inmates of the workhouse and the children from the charity school used to sit up in the gallery.

Fairs were held in May and October. The Horse Fairs took place on the Plains where there were also nutstands and sweet stalls, sellers of harness, brushes, umbrellas, etc. and there were swing boats for children. In 1890 the principal exhibitors of horses were Mr. Shinner from Stretchford, Staverton, and Mr. Barrett from Puddaven.

Each town possessed a lock-up or prison; there was one at Totnes Guildhall and one in Bridgetown. At the Guildhall, there was a walled-up area behind which the prisoners could wash. In 1890 the old Grammar School was purchased by the Town Council and the building used for police quarters and prison cells—the old ones being considered unsuitable.

The houses in Warland were built on a 13th century dam constructed between Ticklemore Street and the St. Peter's Quay area and were always prone to flooding. Mr. George Westaway, with his son, still operates the forge at No. 27 as did his father before him. Blight, the carter, stabled his horses nearby.

The True Street toll house (of the Totnes and Bridgetown Pomeroy Turnpike Trust) was sold with another toll house for £120 in 1881. The house had an unusual round slate-hung front instead of the commoner three-sided one and was pulled down in 1968.

The new toll-bridge over the river was opened in 1828. The tolls from the gates were offered by auction and in 1873 the Totnes Bridge gate fetched £421. When the powers of the Turnpike Trust expired at midnight on 1st November, 1881, there was great excitement, the gates were publicly burnt and a torch light procession went round the town.

Horses crossing the river at Totnes Races. The course ran from Bourton Hall — now Chateau Bellevue — round the quarry alongside the Newton Abbot road, down the bank past the ropewalk and over the Dart to the finish. Crossing the river could be a very hazardous affair especially when the river was in flood.

The Annual Race Meeting at Totnes, held in September, was such a popular and fashionable event that great crowds attended and in Edwardian days the meeting earned the title of "Derby of the West". The stands and stewards' enclosure, especially, were patronised by the "elite" of the district. Race-goers came by train, horse transport, cars and on foot.

A Bowling Club match against Torquay in 1909. *Top row:* Dr. R. P. Jellicoe (*on left*). The Totnes team (*in second row*) L. to r.: H. Worth, H. Maddick, Ed. Tucker, S. Stiggins, F. T. Tucker, G. H. Kirk, W. H. Nugent, F. T. Hannaford. C. W. Vibert.

The Royal 1st Devon Imperial Yeomanry Territorial Force on Church Parade. Sergeant-major W. H. Seale, the drill instructor, lived in Maudlin Road in 1910.

The great fire of 1905 involved Haymans, Meltons, Stoyles and Reeves in High Street and the damage was estimated at £20,000. The fire raged for several hours and threatened to destroy the centre of the town including the Butterwalk on the other side. The fire engine took 15 minutes to get up steam and a special train brought the Exeter brigade within an hour.

Almshouses, originally built on the Plains in 1602, were removed to the Grove in 1832 and re-built on the site of the former Carrion Pits. They bore a plaque with the words "Remember the poore. God will remember thee". The buildings were demolished, and replaced by old people's houses in 1979.

On Coronation Day in 1902, Totnes was thoroughly "en fete" and there were large numbers of people about to admire and to criticise the efforts of those who displayed tokens of loyalty to the Crown (as here in Fore Street). The day's festivities ended with a grand promenade concert, fireworks and an "al fresco" ball on the Island.

The decorations for Edward VII's coronation were described as "a beautiful spectacle worthy of the ancient Borough and the subject of admiration by every visitor who came into the town". The Castle Hotel (Mrs. Blight's) was bright with King and Queen bunting, artificial flowers, portraits of the King and Queen, shields, evergreens and E.R. in fairy lights.

"Mr. F. T. Tucker's residence (in High Street) was festooned with large paper roses and bunting, interspersed with flags. A number of fairy lights were hanging along the top of the building. The choice flowers in the window added to Miss Goodman's display." *Totnes Times, August 1902.*

Ashford Slip and Riding Place Quay was the ancient ford of the Dart which had been put out of use when the island was extended northwards to abut the bridge and to increase the flow of water down the mill leat. The store on the left was used by Symons' Cider Company and is now Crook's Garage.

A carnival float for Symons' Cider. Messrs. John Symons and Co. alleged that they were makers of the finest cider that ever came out of the West Country. They were large employers of labour and offered prizes for the best kept apple orchards in the district. In the autumn the smell of apples pervaded the Plains when cider making was in progress.

The bearded figure on the right is Thomas Creaser Kellock who lived at Highfield and was Mayor of Totnes in 1865, 1884, 1885 and 1896. He is here seen walking down the road past the Kingsbridge Inn. A keen photographer can be seen on the left of the picture.

Livestock being herded to and from their pastures or to market was a common sight. The livestock market was held on the first and third Tuesday of each month at the top of the town, between Cistern Street and Leechwell Gardens, until the new market was opened on the Industrial Estate by the Queen in 1962.

General Sir William Birdwood visits Totnes on 24th August, 1919, to receive the Honorary Freedom of the Borough. He was the sixth member of his family to receive the Freedom and chose the title Baron Birdwood of Anzac and Totnes, when he was raised to the peerage. Birdwood gained lasting fame at Gallipoli—his example was such an inspiration to the Australian and New Zealand Forces that they named him "The Soul of Anzac".

The Market House Inn porch. There was a continuous line of buildings down South Street before the present Civic Hall was built. Rooms attached to the old Shambles Gate (later the Market House Inn) led into the market. The buildings were demolished in 1959.

High Street with Thomas, the tailors, Edgcumbe and Sons, outfitters, and Tuckers on the right. Tuckers were established in 1808 and were Wholesale and Retail Grocers, Tea Merchants. They were also makers of Orange Marmalade, Jams, Totnes Butter Scotch and Cream Toffees. Soft fruit for the jam factory, behind the shop, travelled by train in barrels with sacking to cover them.

King William IV Hotel shortly before demolition and rebuilding in 1902; in those days it was a combined hotel, travellers' resting place and omnibus depot. The fare from Totnes to Paignton was 1/- each way. The sign on the wall warns cyclists to ride with caution.

Looking down river from the bridge, one can see the warehouses on the Bridgetown side which were built by the 11th Duke of Somerset (1775-1855) who was instrumental in setting up the River Dart Navigation Commission in 1834. The coming of the railway took away much of the coal and heavy traffic from the river but there was still quite a lot of river trade towards the end of the century.

The house on the corner on the left, built as a private house in 1836, later became the Corner House Cafe. The first Post Office was at No. 1 Fore Street at the beginning of this century and the National Telephone Company's call office was at No. 6. The Town Arms at 15 Fore Street had a harness room with stabling and accommodation for grooms and stable boys at the rear.

Mill Lane and Mill Cottage. This narrow lane, which led alongside the Seven Stars Hotel (and still does), was the only direct access to the North from the Plains until Coronation Road was constructed in 1937. Manor House, formerly called the (lay) Rectory, is hidden behind the line of trees.

These splendid bicycles were shown at the Jubilee celebrations in 1897. The *Totnes Times* reported that there was "a striking contrast between 1837, represented by Mr. H. Jordan, mounted on a "bone-shaker", and 1897 as depicted by Mr. Soul riding a "modern safety"."

Mr. Baldwin opened his garage in Station Road in 1923 after having worked with Thorneycrofts at Basingstoke. The petrol pump was one of the few in the district and Baldwins were agents for Morris Motors. Jack Treby, an insurance agent from Harbertonford, drove into Totnes every day on his motor bike and side car (foreground).

An outing from the King William IV pub c. 1924 with: *Rear* V. Parnell, N. Harding, J. Knapman, J. A. Whiteway, A. Crook, James. *Seated* F. Dash, Richardson, B. Eames, —. Eames, Churchward, B. Kendall. *Standing* A. Venton, Waldron (painter and decorator), Stoneman, Yeoman (gas company worker), "Punch"!, G. Pack, Arscott (sign writer), Mills (mason), Potter (Blight's carter).

Inspection of the Totnes Division of the Red Cross at Flete on 3rd June, 1914. Fifteen minutes was allowed for giving First Aid and setting up a 19-bed field hospital; all equipment, except stretchers, was sent from Totnes; the wounded were represented by Boy Scouts. Each detachment had its own primus stove and biscuit tin kitchen.

The Armistice, 11th November, 1918. A few minutes after the official notice appeared in the *Totnes Times* window, flags and streamers were everywhere. A mass meeting was hastily organised by the Mayor and included the Corporation, the Borough Band (which sprang into existence within an hour) and convalescent soldiers and nursing staff from the voluntary hospital at Follaton House.

The Dart Valley Spitfire £5,000 Fund was oversubscribed by £150 in April, 1941, and by dint of linking up Totnes, Dartmouth and Kingswear the district was enabled to have a fighter of its own. Great credit was due to the Mayor, Alderman Edgcumbe, the Borough's "Chief Spitfire", who worked assiduously to achieve the target.

Fore Street in 1910. Mrs. F. T. Willis's fancy repository at No. 58 was noted for picture postcards; opposite Kellow's restaurant was the Vicarage (later the Borough Council offices). The Y.M.C.A. was in the Windeatt Hall behind 67 and Mrs. Ellen Doble kept apartments at 74. Henry Kinsman kept the East Gate Inn at 71 (two doors below the East Gate).

The *Margaret and Ann, Rye* moored alongside the Long Marsh. The targets of the rifle range in the background were used by the Volunteers "C" Company. Their armoury was in the large hall (now the Library) in the 1900s and on Monday evenings the Volunteers paraded to the range for practice headed by their band. A red flag was flown at Windwhistle Cottage during practice.

Castle Street with North Gate in the background. There were numerous bill-posting stations around the town, the poster on the wall is advertising Sully's Drapery Sale. Miss E. Sully ran a Fancy Drapers at 62 High Street in 1907.

Follaton Lodge and Follaton Avenue in the background. The avenue of trees was cut down to allow for the ribbon development along Higher Plymouth Road; many local people took their walks along the Avenue on Sunday afternoons.

Miss Pinn's School c. 1919. Totnes Girls' School was established in 1884 over Mrs. Worth's music shop at 35 Fore Street by Miss Windeatt (who was considered most daring when she attended lectures on physiology as it was thought improper for ladies to see bones and skeletons). The school is remembered as Miss Pinn's, as she was a co-founder of it.

The stocks were alleged to have been sited in the old Church Walk where they could be seen by all passers-by. This photograph was taken outside the Guildhall where the stocks are now housed. A report of 1897 stated that the stocks had still been in use 60 years previously.

21

A view looking down Fore Street shows Mrs. Kellow's Refreshment Rooms at No. 60; Heal's the tobacconists at 62 also had a wheelwright's shop in the Grove; Nicholas Adams, stationer at 64, was clerk to the Totnes Cemetery Committee in 1910. Gas lighting was installed in the town in 1837.

Before the First World War there was a Picturedrome at the Seymour Hotel with an entrance fee of one penny to see the silent movies. At the piano was Miss Seaward. Hotel prices fluctuated considerably after the war. In the early 1920s, prices at the Seymour were: Room, single 4/-, double 6/-, breakfast 2/6, dinner 4/-. Boarding terms were from 8/6 per day.

The grounds of Totnes Castle had been laid out and planted as a promenade for the public by the Duke of Somerset in 1844. It was a grand venue for fetes, with maypole dancers, fireworks, archery, quoits etc., even in 1860, an amateur band of Ethiopian dancers! The Ministry of Works took over the castle in 1947.

This donkey accompanied by a small boy was employed at the end of the 19th century to deliver bread from the bakery of Mrs. Tuckett who ran the business with her two daughters at 5 Fore Street. On Sundays there would have been a procession of people going to the bakers to get their dinners cooked in the big ovens.

Girls in Church School play in the 1920s

Back row: A. Norsworthy, D. Libby, T. Philot, G. Trembath, L. Gregory, O. Boyce, E. Waldron, M. Lucas, M. Medhurst, D. Dowell, J. Prior. *Middle Row:* M. Tapley, P. Trembath, E. Harris, F. Easterbrook, N. Bickford, E. Stevens, L. Yeoman, F. Tapley, M. Hoopell, T. Cranwell, D. Blatchford, —, D. Shillabeer, F. Hayman. *Seated:* M. Stoyle, I. Sherriff, E. Beer, K. Rice, M. Relland, E. Dowell, N. Knapman, E. Hodge, V. Yeoman, P. Matters, C. Nott, H. Gill, G. Doble, I. Perring, S. Fisher, E. Bowhay.

The Narrows in 1924. Harris and Sons at 92 and 99 High Street were general and agricultural ironmongers and implement dealers, also shoeing and general smiths. On the left hand side, below Collins Corner, was the Plymouth Inn and, below that, Bate and Co. (proprietors Le Duc) at the West End Stores. On the right was Hunts sweetshop—Jordans bicycle shop was at 94 High Street.

Midsummer Night's Dream at King Edward VI School, 1925. *Standing L to r:* Binnie Barrett, Ed. Tucker, Royce Frost, George Heath, Frank Jordan, Jack Robjohns. *Sitting, middle:* Douglas Hudson, Hamlyn Parsons, Louis Scoble, Clarence Tinney, Alfred(?) Trembath.

The Traffic Warden's job was not to deal with parking offenders (as now) but to control traffic. He stood in the corner of the Narrows to direct the two-way flow of traffic up and down the street and the vehicles going in and out of Tuckers Sweet Factory (now Castle Court).

An unusual sight of the river frozen over in January, 1963. Mr. Togo Brook of the Dart Navigation Commissioners reported that a timber boat, being piloted up to Totnes, had to plough through ice floes 2 ins deep in the Home Reaches. A number of people were able to skate on the river above the weir.

Arthur L. Clamp – the man behind the books

Arthur Leslie Clamp was a man of boundless energy with a passion for helping others, particularly through his love of history. A printer by trade, he started his career in a printing company before moving his family from Exeter to Plymouth to teach at the Plymouth College of Art and Design, where he eventually became the Head of the Printing Department.

A Devoted Family Man

Arthur with his five children.

Despite his love of teaching, Arthur prioritised his family, always making it home by 5:30pm for tea. He and his wife, Rosemary, raised five children: Susan, Angela, Elizabeth, David, and Steven. Arthur would often combine his love of family and history by taking his children on Sunday walks, encouraging them to appreciate historical monuments by taking photos or making crayon rubbings of gravestones for his books. The family home at 203 Elburton Road was a hub of activity, with a large garden, featuring a two-storey fort and a makeshift swimming pool.

A Lifelong Learner and Adventurer

Arthur's thirst for knowledge extended beyond history to a deep curiosity about the world. He was passionate about exploring different cultures, traditions, and cuisines, often taking advantage of his long summer holidays as a teacher to travel to places like India, Russia, South America, the middle east and the USA, sometimes bringing one of his children along. This adventurous spirit even influenced his home life, as seen by the short-lived family tradition of steam-cooking vegetables after a trip to Iceland.

History is a prominent feature of family days out

Community and Philanthropic Spirit

His commitment to serving others was evident in his long-standing involvement with the Elburton Methodist Church. He was the Sunday School Superintendent for over 15 years and served as the editor of the wider church's monthly newsletter, "The Link," for a similar duration. After Rosemary's very sad passing, Arthur later remarried and, following a chance encounter with a professor from India, established a connection with a missionary school in Chennai. Together with his new wife, Christine, he co-founded a "Sponsor a Child's Education" program that continues to this day.

Pictured left – The cover of 'The Link' complete with hand drawn sketches of each church by Angela
Below right – Arthur Clamp promoting his latest book
Below left – Arthur at home with his first wife, Rosemary
Below centre – Arthur on holiday with his second wife, Christine

A Legacy of Learning and Positivity

Arthur's greatest passion was history, which he brought to life through tireless research, documentation, and the many books he authored. He was driven by a need to "never be stuck in a rut," constantly seeking new experiences, meeting new people, and expanding his knowledge. With a positive attitude and a great sense of humour, he was always ready to help others, leaving a lasting impact on his family and community. His children, Susan, Angela, Elizabeth, David, and Steven, remember him with love and gratitude.

David Clamp, 2025

A Legacy of Local History

Below is the story of how Arthur L Clamp began writing books, in his own words, drafted shortly before he passed away in 2001. I have only made minor alterations to this text, correcting grammatical errors that he did not survive to correct himself. When I first discovered this text, I was shocked to see my name mentioned. It seems that, unbeknownst to me, I shared my first PC with him. I suspect he used it during the day when I was at school, although I do have one memory of sitting with him and showing him how it worked. It has been a pleasure to pick up where he left off and see his books republished and redistributed, and to know that I was part of the story, even back then. It was also fascinating to discover that his pricing structure matches the way I have tried to price the books, with a third going to local sellers and the rest covering printing costs with a little left over for my expenses.

I am his eldest grandson, and it is a privilege to curate his legacy, which we are calling 'The Clamp Collection'. The very last line of the text originally reads "The following pages list all the titles." Sadly, that page is missing and we have no record of all the books he published and knowing that some of those were researched by other authors makes the process of finding them even harder. I look forward to one day completing the collection and seeing them all available again. And maybe, one day, I'll even start writing my own to add to the series. For now, here is his story in his own words.

Steven Gibson, 2025

Writing and Publishing Booklets on Local Topics and Areas

I started this interest in either 1968 or 1969 when living in Woodford. I had by these dates established the Department of Printing and I think I must have been looking for something different to do. The first titles were of A5 size proofed from type set at Clarke, Doble and Brendon, Ltd., Plymouth printers, and then made up into pages and printed at Sawtell and Neilson, Ltd., Totnes.

Then began a slow process of getting them out to shops, etc. which proved to be more time consuming and difficult than actually researching, writing and getting the books into print. However, I persisted and opened a business account with Barclays Bank on the Broadway. I was advised to give it a title so I called it "Westway Publications". There came along another problem, one of storage of paper and finished books which was solved when the family moved to Elburton in 1970.

I changed the printer to Penwell, Ltd., Callington, Cornwall, as he was then just setting up himself and his prices seemed very reasonable. I did not get any of the printers to make up the complete books. I hand folded the flat printed sheets, stitched the books on a small manual table stitcher and trimmed them in a small hand turned guillotine which I bought from someone in Penzance for £40. It was brought up in a van.

The trouble and time going to and fro to Callington was too much so I transferred the printing to PDS Printers, Prince Rock, Plymouth, and I have been with them ever since. Now they are at Plympton which is easy to reach and they fold the flat sheets which was turning out to be a long chore which only saved a small part of the printing costs.

All my first titles were written by myself. I took the photographs and developed them in the loft of the house, the type was set by now on a computer situated in the house at Elburton from which I had collected photographic lengths of text to cut up and law down as pages.

At some point I decided that I would do my own film processing of lith film so I bought a large second hand process camera from Kingsbridge and learnt through trial and error to make line negatives of the text and halftone negatives of the illustrations which proved more difficult than I anticipated. The main problem was trying to keep the developer in the large dish at the correct temperature as any change would affect the developing time. I replaced this old camera with a brand new one bought from Croydon, Surrey, costing £900. This has turned out to be a great asset cutting out an expensive part of the printer's costs and one crucial aspect of the work which I could control.

By the middle 1970s there were many outlets I had contacted in Plymouth, up to Dartmoor, Exeter, around to Torbay, Totnes, Dartmouth and the South Hams. The market for local books was much greater than I had first thought and through getting to know many local people undertaking research themselves had the chance to help and make up books for other people who had in most instances, got together a collection of photographs with some text in a rather muddled way. Through my experience in print I was able to shape up their work and get it into print and in every case I had to pay the printer and let the person have the royalties. In the majority of titles produced in this manner this was another way of producing titles and it did give some profit to my work. However, I must say that in a few cases I lost out by either the other person getting the numbers wrong, not returning any monies from stock I delivered or they thought that more of their books should have been sold.

The print run was usually 1,000 copies and from time to time I have had reprints of 250 copies. It took about ten years to clear the first print run so I always had large stocks in the garage, workshop, etc. The numbers sold during the early years was about 7,000 copies a year increasing to around 9,000 copies and for the whole of the enterprise about 500,000 have been sold. The booklets have become part of the local scene and many people collect them, shops regularly order copies and I go around certain areas month by month restocking or replacing titles as necessary.

During the past year or so I have started setting the text on a Packard Bell PC, something which I should have done some years back. I share it with Steven Gibson, my grandson. There appears to be no end to the market for local books, but I could not earn a regular income because of the long time it takes to sell stock.

However, now exceeding 100 titles made up mainly of A4 twenty-four page booklets, some folded guides, with selling prices set with a third going to the shop which is the trade custom, the original idea has been quite successful and could go on for ever.

Apart from monetary benefits, however spasmodically these might be, I have learnt a lot myself, met many interesting people and have become part of the local scene with requests to give talks and to advise people about getting into print.

Arthur L Clamp, 2001

This newspaper article, published by the Evening Herald on 17th August 2001, forms a good record of his life. Just as he encourages us to learn more about local history, we encourage you to learn a little about him. For that reason, we have included these pages at the back of all the most recently republished books, in honour of his memory and recognition of his contribution to the community.

www.ingramcontent.com/pod-product-compliance
Lightning Source LLC
Chambersburg PA
CBHW061409070526
44584CB00031B/4193